Creating Your Own Strength
Self-Love

"Strength shows, not only in the ability to persist, but the ability to start over."

Copyright © 2019
Creating **Y**our **O**wn **S**trength
Self-**L**ove

Nivlac the Brand

Nivlac_thebrand@yahoo.com
Nivlac_thebrand (Facebook)
Nivlac_thebrand (Twitter)
Nivlac_thebrand (Instagram)

ALL RIGHTS RESERVED. This book contains material protected under International and Federal Copyright Laws and Treaties. Any unauthorized reprint or use of this material is prohibited. All names and places in this book has been fictionalized. No part of this book may be reproduced or transmitted in any form or by any means, electronic or mechanical, including photocopying, recording, or by any information storage and retrieval system without express written permission from the author/publisher. This book is Fiction and because of the dynamic nature of content.

ISBN: 9781680260694

Dedication:
To My Beloved Grandmother
Ms. Rosa Cox

Table of Contents

Foreword By Tina Marie vii

Prologue xi

Chapter 1 - Flames and Feelings 1

Chapter 2 - The TV Show 10

Chapter 3 - Dancing with the Stars 18

Chapter 4 - Growing Pains 22

Chapter 5 - People Under the Stairs 30

Chapter 6 - The Half and the Half Not
              Siblings 37

Chapter 7 - 450 Gilbert 60

Chapter 8 - What Lies Beneath 67

Chapter 9 - The New Change 74

Chapter 10 - Grown and Sexy 78

Chapter 11 - Face to Face 82

Chapter 13 - Lord of the Rings Spirit of the
              Hidden Devil 97

Chapter 14 - Creating a New Strength 106

Chapter 15 - Don't Get Caught Up 116

Epilogue

Closing Remarks 122

Know Your Self-worth..................... 122

Foreword

By Tina Marie

I have watched Nivlac work hard to become an independent and educated man who is following his dreams and going against all odds to prove he is enough. Nivlac has always maintained a certain level of privacy to protect his peace, but in doing so, he never made me feel like I did not know him or that I could not trust him. He has always been a selfless person who is thoughtful, respectful and nurturing to those he cares about.

Over the years, Nivlac and I have shared bits and pieces about our childhood and some of the trauma we endured. He made it so easy for me to be transparent about the things I went through, and he never judged me or made me feel uncomfortable in sharing my experiences. Nivlac encouraged me to pursue my goal of writing a book to share my story. I believe somewhere along the way, him encouraging many others and me inspired him to practice what he preaches.

This is how our phone conversations go ring ring… "Hey Nivlac, this is Tina, what are you doing this weekend? We need you to dog sit Kayne!" "Tina you know I will do anything for you and Shrek, but I'm entertaining some friends at my place this weekend hunty!" "Well kill two birds with one stone and host your gathering at our house and watch Kayne at the same time!" "Girl please, your house is so small hunty I can sneeze in the kitchen and stretch my arm out to grab toilet paper from the bathroom! My friends will be like, are we being punked?" We both erupt with laughter and his laugh makes me laugh harder and then come the tears because once Nivlac gets started there's no stopping him and its comedy central until we're all laughed out!

I am so proud of Nivlac for this leap of faith in sharing his story. There are so many people who still don't understand the who, why, where, and what went WRONG in their life, and I strongly feel Creating Your Own Strength (Self-Love) will touch lives and empower many people all over the world who need to hear Nivlac's story of finding self-worth and creating his own strength on his journey to self-love.

They say, "Good friends are hard to find!" Well, thank God I did not have to look for Nivlac because he was indeed a Godsend. We met via a mutual acquaintance, and our chemistry was so powerful, we instantly bonded and grew very close in such a short time. In the twenty-three years, we have been friends, our respect, loyalty, and support for each other has deepened our bond and brought us much closer than friends. Permanently, Nivlac is my friend, my confidant, my comedian, my chef, my encourager and my little brother from another mother. I am enjoying reading this book **Creating Your Own Strength** I am sure you will as well.

Prologue

I have learned to accept the fact that in life everyone will one day disappoint you at some point in your life. Prepare yourself mentally and physically to be hurt, disappointed, being lied on, bullied, scared, lonely, or abused by some people you love. I have carried shame, guilt, pain, and hopelessness for most of my life. I have learned to depend on my intuition and Self-Love. I am now releasing any pain that has caused me to feel less of a person and bitterness. I am **CREATING MY OWN STRENGTH.** By praying to God and knowing that my good days will outnumber my bad days. I grew up shy and felt alone most of my life, despite having a large family I was still the only child. In my adult life, I had to depend on my friends' families for holidays, birthdays and special occasions to feel as if it was my family. Just to go home and cry in my pillow wondering why I do not have any sisters or brothers who lived with me. Why does a child have both parents but not really close to any of them growing up? This kind of lifestyle I did not ask for, why didn't my parents teach me about sex? Why did I have to reach out to them when I was alone or hungry. I love my parents, but my Granny was my number one. I completed high school, got my diploma, and went to a few trade schools in between. I obtained my bachelor's degree in my thirties, in Atlanta Georgia, where I now reside. Working full time and living a middle-class life just is not enough for me. Not having any kids to leave my legacy, I wrote this book as things inspired me to change my life. Having a strong personality people always gravitated to me all ages, races, colors, and religions. From the people I met as friends, coworkers, family and strangers, I have influenced most of their lives in one way or another. I am a non-judgmental person I believe what you put out you will get in return. I try to treat people with kindness and be open-minded but as an adult, I have had my share of bad tempers and plenty of altercations. I learned how to cook from my Granny, and I am very good at it. My cookbook or cookbook calendar is coming soon along with other things I aspire to achieve. Nivlac is very easy to please I love going to the movies, shopping and traveling. Some feel I am an Icon when it comes to fashion, because I create my fashion looks. I decided to start my brand in spring 2020. Note from the author Calvin Hill, if you are reading this book. Know that anything is possible, and keep your ideas and hope alive. Believe in God and process all bad and good information with the best possible outcome for yourself. Creating Your Own Strength is for everyone to find self-love and much happiness.

    This is a book about events and situations inspired by my life and an introduction to real-life conditions. The character's name is Nivlac; he grew up knowing that he was special in some way shape, form or fashion. This book is about situations that made him the man he is today. There was a time where Nivlac was a very shy little boy who was bullied and ashamed. Then after finding himself through self-love and respect, he became unstoppable and very independent at a young age. Nivlac's favorite color is RED and his favorite number is six. He was born the only child and had two more siblings from his mother and father. His mother got pregnant two times right after him and did not make it to human life. Nivlac never really felt alone until he was alone. His mother showed him how to get on his knees and pray to GOD every night. This is what has kept him all these years and God been along his side since day one through the good and the bad.

Chapter 1

Flames and Feelings

Nivlac was packing his things to move back to Grand Rapids, Michigan from Atlanta, Georgia in 1999. He relocated to start a new life with new goals. He was only in Atlanta two months; the day skin melted off his body. As he was pondering how to get rid of a car, he had bought in Michigan that broke down on the drive to Atlanta when the transmission went out. The car was not reliable for Atlanta highways and streets. Nivlac visited Atlanta, over the years and liked it he ended up driving a car that he bought from his stepmother Bernice's friend Stacy who sold him her Lexus, but on the way to

Atlanta, the transmission blew out. Nivlac had a friend named Berry, who traveled to Michigan to help drive to Atlanta. When the car broke down, Nivlac had to get it towed from Tennessee to Atlanta after panicking from the smoke and engine locked up. When Nivlac encountered the unexpected car failure, he moved in with Berry, who was his best friend at the time. Nivlac and Berry started working together and carpooled to work as well. Nivlac felt defeated again, trying to make a better life for himself and once again, something happened to change his life. During the transmission going out, Nivlac's father Ralph had a cousin named Lenard, who knew a shade tree mechanic that could fix his broke down Lexus for a little of nothing. Prior to this untimely car failure, Nivlac is reminded of when he went to the car lot before moving from Michigan and asked his father Ralph to co-sign for him a new car, a green Chevy Cavalier to be exact, because his intuition told him that the Lexus was going to give out sooner than expected. Nivlac was very disappointed when Ralph denied cosigning.

Nivlac's disappointment in Ralph's no to cosign was due more to Ralph knowing the Lexus Nivlac bought was not dependable and would eventually give out. Nivlac felt Ralph knew he would need reliable transportation to drive out of state. A result of his car troubles, Nivlac decided to move back to Michigan and regroup. Berry asked Nivlac, "Are you moving back to Michigan." Nivlac said, "Yeah we no longer work at the same job and I have no way to work." Nivlac went back to Michigan to get his friends Chase and Bernard. They accompanied Nivlac back to Atlanta to help him move his things. Nivlac rented a van from Michigan to drive to Atlanta. The van was big enough to accommodate Chase,

Bernard, Nivlac and his belongings.

Berry told Nivlac one of his friends got rid of a few cars before and this information gave Nivlac the motivation to do something illegal. One day Nivlac presented the idea of getting rid of the Lexus to Ralph. Nivlac suggested driving the Lexus somewhere. To burn it and leave it where no one could see the flames. Nivlac explained to Ralph how they could make an insurance claim and use the money to get another car. Nivlac went into a gas station in Decatur, Georgia where he lived for a few months with his friend Berry. Nivlac bought a gas can, filled it with gas, and drove to an abandoned parking lot where he had parked the Lexus. Bernard was with him, because Nivlac asked him to ride along while he burned the Lexus. As Nivlac poured gas all over the car and in the car, the fumes from the gas were strong.

Nivlac was wondering if he should follow

through with this because he knew the flames would attract attention. As he lit the car on fire, he forgot to get the license plate off, so he started to do that and then remembered he forgot to get the registration and insurance papers from the glove box. The car was on FIRE, but at this point, he thought he had time to grab the stuff and go. During the Lexus burning, Nivlac suffered second-degree burns on his face, arms, and legs; the skin wilted like plastic. They considered this 2nd-degree burns which Nivlac now has tattooed over his legs. He rushed back to his friend Berry's house in Decatur and called his Granny. Nivlac did not share the extinct of his burns; he just said he was in an accident. Granny suggested he take a cold shower. Nivlac immediately went into shock, as he was on a stretcher in the hallway of the hospital for an hour in pain, with no pain meds or no room.

The pain was unbearable he remembers looking up and the doctors were pulling his skin off his arms and legs saying it will heal better that way. Nivlac suffered from second-degree burns and they had to remove the skin off his body. The pain was so horrible he cried wishing he were dead, contemplating on if he could walk to the hospital room window he could jump. How can his life come to this? His face suffered burns not as bad as the other parts of the body. He was in the hospital under an alias so that the police would not link him to the Lexus he burned. Nivlac called home to his family and told them what was going on and what had happened, and they were devastated. He also told his distant cousin Tangie, who lived in Atlanta what really happened. As he laid there approximately four days with bandages on his legs and arms, with half of his face discolored, Nivlac was grateful his Aunt Melia was asking family to get up the money for her to fly to Atlanta and be by his side. Nivlac had no family in Atlanta, and unfortunately the friends he considered family, had to drive back to Michigan and return the rental van and return to work. While Nivlac laid in his hospital bed waiting to return home to Michigan, he will never forget what his stepmother Bernice told him over the phone. Her words were exact, "I don't know where you're going when you get out of the hospital, but you not coming here," which was she and Ralph's home. Nivlac called his best friend Thorey and told him what she said, and Thorey was in disbelief and so upset. Nivlac knew better than to share this with his aunts aka his protectors, because he knew the outcome was not going to be nice. Nivlac was in the hospital Burn Unit learning to walk and use his arms and legs again with continued weeks of therapy. The day of his release from the hospital Nivlac's friend Berry took him to the airport, and he traveled back to Grand Rapids, Michigan. Once Nivlac arrived in Michigan, he was so embarrassed he had to wear bandages on both arms and legs. The people at his job teased him by calling him Richard Pryor, because of how he burned himself up. Some of the humor was all in fun but others tried to hurt him. Nivlac wore bandages on his legs and arms for another six months and was scared to go out in public because people would stare. Nivlac's face healed first, thank GOD. His primary physician in Michigan advised Nivlac to let the air hit the wound so it could heal and form new skin. Although Bernice initially said Nivlac could not stay in the home she shared with Ralph, her heart softened, and after living in their home for a few weeks, Nivlac moved from couch to couch in the home of others for about two months. His Aunt Melia invited him to live with her and her daughter in a one bedroom until he got himself together. Then Nivlac met E.H. who was so infatuated with him. Nivlac was still able to go out and hide his scars, because it was cold enough in Michigan during that time, and was common to wear long sleeve shirt or pants. Nivlac's face healed very fast so bandages wasn't needed to cover his face.

Chapter 2
The TV Show

Nivlac and his mom Jeanie were living at 730 Bates Street in Grand Rapids, Michigan, and while watching TV together, a show came on with a white mom and her daughter. Nivlac would never forget this day when he was around the age of nine or ten years old. The show was about a young girl and her molestation. After the scene of the daughter telling her mom she was molested and identifying her molester, Jeanie turned to Nivlac and asked, "Has anyone ever touched you? You better tell me." Nivlac immediately went into the bathroom looked in the mirror and said to himself I'm about to tell her. After crying in the mirror and being ashamed and scared at the same time, he was so nervous when he made it back to the living room. Nivlac was truthful and said, "Yeah by my uncle, your brother." Jeanie turned on the light made a big scene crying and mad calling Aunt Bubba, who lived in an apartment in front of their apartment. She left Nivlac with Aunt Bubba about an hour later Ralph came and picked him up. During that hour, Aunt Bubba looked at his butt and asked Nivlac, "What did he do to you?" Nivlac was unsure he just knew he used have a wet butt.

Ralph took Nivlac to his apartment on Dorris Street, which was upstairs from his Aunt VI DoDo, and gave him his favorite snack, hostess chocolate cupcakes, and juice. Ralph sat with Nivlac on the couch, but Nivlac doesn't recall Ralph asking him any questions or doing anything to help, and if he did, he kept Nivlac out of it. Nivlac heard Jeanie confront his uncle, fighting and screaming at him, but for the most part, Nivlac was left in the dark about the situation. People use to ask him what happened, but Nivlac never liked to speak on it, because he doesn't think it was penetration. He just remembers being wet on his butt from the molester rubbing his penis on it. At some point, Nivlac thought he liked it even though he knew it was wrong, but the uncle and Nivlac were close, so he never threatened Nivlac, he just assumed Nivlac would not say anything to anyone.

    Nivlac also had cousins who humped on him with clothes on and he never spoke on that either, because he assumed that what happens in black families. Nivlac was very shy as a child but very bad, and he talked back to adults. Nivlac's behavior was so bad, he would fall out on the ground and embarrassed Jeanie in front of friends and family numerous times. The elders always told Jeanie she needed to whoop his bad ass. However, Jeanie never let anybody put his or her hands on her son, her baby.

One day Jeanie tried to whoop him with a belt and Nivlac took the belt and hit her with it. Her friend Charlie Roberts fell out laughing and uttered, "How the hell you given out a whooping and he take the belt."

Jeanie owned two houses; her and Nivlac lived in one and rented the second property. Nivlac had all the toys and games he wanted and was very spoiled. All his cousins used to come to stay at his house, so he barely got a chance to be the only child. Jeanie had two best friends Suzie and Sharon who had kids of their own, which we considered family. At some point while Nivlac and Jeanie lived on Griggs and Kalamazoo, Jeanie begin hanging out at bars. One bar was Bills Retreat, which was owned by her uncle. During that era, Bills Retreat was a popular bar. One night during Jeanie's bar outing, Nivlac woke up alone and sad crying when he noticed his mom was not in the house. He called his Granny on the phone and told her his mom left him alone in the house again by himself. Nivlac was only six years of age and was scared. He noticed a shadow as he looked in her closet, so he immediately got on his knees to pray like his mom taught him every night. His Granny was so upset she cursed Jeanie out about leaving him home alone. Jeanie's bar outings led to Nivlac often staying at his Granny's house, and with unlimited supervision, Nivlac was being molested, upstairs while his grandparents were asleep.

Jeanie tried to give Nivlac a whooping, another time and started crying because she could not do it. Nivlac continued his bad behavior despite being bullied in school from kindergarten through second grade. Due to the bullying, when Nivlac begin Camp Paul Elementary, Jeanie put him in karate class, and she walked him to the bus stops. Nivlac parents would also make school visits to check on him.

Ralph and Jeanie met at South High School and Ralph was a grade or two ahead of Jeanie. Jeanie was a pretty girl with good hair and pretty skin they called her Jeanie which was her nickname. Ralph was a soldier who served in the military. Nivlac was born Thanksgiving night at 12:03am when Jeanie went into labor after eating Aunt Isis sweet potato pie. Ralph was visiting Louisiana he did that every year for Thanksgiving, so he was not present for his birth and therefore did not sign his birth certificate.

Nivlac named after his father and his middle name is Shon after some man on the soap opera. His parents were together for a while until Ralph started cheating with another woman. Ralph had an affair with Patty who is Nivlac's, Sister Orange's mom. Oranges was born four months after Nivlac. Ralph married Patty, but after a few months, they were divorced.

Orange got child support until she was eighteen, equal benefits and more than him, her whole life. Nivlac never understood how a parent could show favor towards one child and not the other. Nivlac assumed they were both supposed to be equal with equal love and support. His whole life Nivlac felt like the cousin because he would always have to call Ralph for money. Ralph would give Nivlac and Jeanie money, after a long lecture and inquiry on why it was needed. It was never a lot of money, just enough to get by. One day Ralph told Nivlac and Oranges that he would open them a bank account in their names. Ralph opened Oranges account but never opened one for Nivlac. This inequality caused pain that Nivlac would keep to himself.

This chapter is not to blast his parents or hate them it's the truth and Nivlac is leaving out

several things that occurred out of respect of his parents. You can stop reading now if you feel offended.

Once in middle school, Nivlac was still shy but people begin to befriend him more, because of the way he dressed and his personality he made friends fast. Nivlac had several girlfriends when he got to high school. He was living in the ghetto with his Granny. Nivlac was now trained on how to curse a mother fucker out or whoop some ass. He became very vocal and popular in high school hanging with Mia Howell. Who was a badass chick, which influenced him to be more intimidating and they became besties. His other best friend Piffany P. was in a gang, and with Nivlac knowing all the kids from the hood he was this shit.

Chapter 3

Dancing with the Stars

Nivlac naturally learned to dance at a young age. His Granny would have parties and people would be dancing and having a good ole time. He was influenced by MTV and BET his favorite dancer was MC Hammer. Nivlac developed a style that was incomparable, and he could move his body as if he had no bones.

Besides dancing around the house with his cousins, he started to dance in street fairs, concerts, for rappers and appearing in videos that aired on BET. Nivlac gets an adrenaline rush when he's on stage. When the beat and bass become one with his soul, he performs like a gift from above. Nivlac starting teaching cheerleaders dance team and private dances for a dance studio. After researching dancer salaries, he just started doing it for fun. Nivlac was in several dance groups, performing across Michigan. His last group called Two-Time consisted of him and two female rappers. They were going to be big, Two-Time added a few additional dancers, Nivlac named them Jazz and Rhythm who were pretty girls but not good dancers. Two-Tone secured a manager to book shows for the group, and during this time, Nivlac met a lot of rappers and other dancers.

While Nivlac was dancing and dealing with the issues, he had at home. Like not having food to eat and in the process of him and his mom being evicted, he met a girl. She was pretty and chocolate her name was Meraja she and Nivlac started dating, so he put his secrets aside to pursue something with her. Nivlac and Meraja met at a college where he had a dance performance with the group Two-Time. Meraja was from Detroit and went to school in Grand Rapids. The weekend Meraja was supposed to spend with Nivlac where he lived with his mother, he was waiting to see her two weeks and when the weekend went by, and Meraja was a no show, Nivlac assumed she was uninterested because he wasn't man enough for her. Nivlac was sad and lost hope for his future wife to be. Nivlac soon learned from one of Meraja's friends that she didn't stand him up, she GOT SHOT in the head. Meraja was killed from a mistaken identity in Detroit, Michigan where she was shot at a convince store. Nivlac didn't even get a chance to say goodbye or go to the funeral. During that time, there were no cell phones only pagers. He was devastated so when people asked him if he'd ever had a girlfriend his response was, "Several but the last one was killed." This is a shame, and Detroit was at one point known as the murder capital of the world.

During Nivlac's school years, he had plenty of girlfriends but never had sex with any of them. His soul and heart desired something different he would lust for. Nivlac's had his share of DL (down low) interactions and has kept many secrets. People would be shocked to know everyone he's had dealings with. Nivlac's way of thinking is every man will mess around with another man, and the percentage of that is 90% accurate.

Chapter 4

Growing Pains

Nivlac grew up in the suburbs, but his teen years were lived in the inner city after him and his mother lost the lavish lifestyle, they were accustomed to. Nivlac has seen it all, one thing about growing up in the urban areas is your family and friends were smoking and drinking before their time. Nivlac would be in bars and clubs at age eighteen and had his birthday party at a bar at nineteen. Most bars require you to be twenty-one for entry. Nivlac has had two stalkers in his lifetime. They both were very scary to know that you had someone watching you or observing your life. Nivlac told his Granny almost everything because she was his confidant.

Nivlac wanted to attend college right after high school; even though he was held back, twice he still graduated with good grades. Trying to go to college was very difficult for when financial aid wouldn't approve his applications because his parents didn't have proof of income and Nivlac mother hadn't worked in twenty years. During the time of college enrollment, the financial advisor asked Nivlac, "How the hell does your Mom live, with no proof of income." Nivlac was under the age of twenty-five and he could never go to college because his mom had no proof of income and his father Ralph told him don't ever put his name on any school stuff. Even though Ralph made very good money he was not paying for Nivlac to attend college and made that very clear. Nivlac ended up at a trade school, ITT Tech, where he attended for a few months but that wasn't his passion, so he dropped out for several reasons and end up owing this institution thousands of dollars, and the IRS took his taxes for several years because of this debt. Nivlac was overwhelmed with trying to attend college and just started working and trying to make a living for himself. Nivlac was affected by his mother having no income to provide for the financial aid. And a father who didn't want to show his income to support the funding for school. Some people say that's the past you're an adult, that's **bullshit** being an adult is reflected on how you were treated and raised as a child. Nivlac childhood was ok, not perfect; he made the best of what he could with the mindset of getting back to the old ways he used to live "lavishly" as a child.

Nivlac, become independent and moved out on his own. At age nineteen and had never asked anyone for help. Ralph would help him get repairs on his car if needed or co-sign for a new car but never paid car notes. Nivlac worked and hustled living in the suburbs of the city. Ralph helped him from time to time and he appreciated the little things he did, like pay car insurance, and was on his medical insurance at work. Nevertheless, in real life was equivalent to a few hundred dollars a year. Nivlac was now in a completely new lifestyle and taught a lot from the ones before him the elders of the community. Nivlac would still come around the hood to visit friends and family it was fun. However, always wondered why none of his people wanted more out of life. Most of his family never had jobs lived off hustling and Granny. This was not Nivlac's destiny and now they kind of look up to him like idol, because the abandoned young man at age nineteen has obtained his own place, car, and money on his own. This is what you call Creating Your Own Strength.

People say the reason Ralph did more for Oranges is because Nivlac was a boy and Oranges was a girl. Nivlac feels like he was a kid who couldn't take care of himself and not only that, he didn't not ask to be here. It is a parent's job to make sure all their children treated equally. In addition, shown the same amount of Love. When parents have their favorite child it should not be as noticeable as it was. Nivlac cried many years and never had to courage to confront his father or say anything. When Nivlac became an adult, he would not hesitate about confronting either of the two parents. Especially for any wrongful activity. He knows the bible says to respect thy mother and the father but they had better dam well respect him also, because Nivlac's strength in God was not to taken for granted and he know who his soul provider and still is. Nivlac was what people thought as spoiled, but he just managed his money and the things he accumulated differently. Nivlac had to be an adult before his time so he always was a step above people his age. Nivlac obtained self-love and confidence on his own. Nivlac was more dependent on his father because his mom was not able to provide. The little she did get she helped him a lot. She was one of his biggest consumers and made sure all her friends went to Nivlac. There were times when Nivlac felt bad about the things he had to do to survive and make a decent living but, in his heart, he knew it was going to be very short-lived. Between him hustling and the little money his dad gave him, he was on the right track.

Nivlac had to wait until he got money and his Granny showed him how to open his bank account. His dad was a good man but was never involved like people think. Nivlac use to lie and say the drug money he made is what his dad gave to him. Nivlac knew he was treated differently, so he would cry and ask his mom why? Jeanie try to assure Nivlac that Ralph took care of them, but

Nivlac thought, if that's true why did we have to call for money all the time and why did you have to through hard times and get on food stamps.

Nivlac and Jeanie lived from place to place never stable, and after her medical condition, she begin substance abuse. Nivlac wasn't aware of Jeanie's substance abuse for the first few years. Nivlac didn't know even know what drugs were or how they change people. Nivlac told his mom Ralph treated him differently than he treated Oranges and Jeanie said, "No he doesn't." Nivlac responded, "Yes he does my sister get everything and I get scraps." Nivlac wasn't complaining because scraps were better than nothing back then. Nevertheless, even as Nivlac grew older he received the same relevancy and money from Ralph that you would give a nephew or niece. On graduation day, he thought he was getting a car but instead, Ralph had him go to the dealership with him to pick up stepmom Bernice's new red Corvette.

Nivlac felt that was a slap in the face, not to mention he never received a graduation gift. Ralph and Bernice hosted an open house for Nivlac and his cousin Dr. Datson at their home and even though Nivlac never received a gift from them, he was grateful they co-hosted a joint open house for him and his cousin.

Chapter 5

People Under the Stairs

Nivlac and Jeanie moved in with his aunts and their boyfriends at 1136 Jefferson where they all had their own rooms. It was Nivlac Grannie's house and their mother she owned it along with several others. After the drug, addiction got worse Nivlac and Jeanie lost so many things and was poor until Jeanie met Dwayne who was nice to her and Nivlac. Dwayne moved Jeanie and Nivlac to Muskegon and she soon begin to steal things from Dwayne, and she sold them to support her habits. Nivlac was so tired of getting things taken from him and not having food or clean clothes to go to school, he ended up held back a grade from missing so much school. Bernice and

Ralph let him stay with them until he finished middle school at Iroquois's.

Nivlac liked Dwayne a lot because he was cool and a provider. Dwayne had a good job and a nice jeep. He was from Muskegon and was divorced with two girls. He would treat Nivlac like one of his kids. Dwayne was a nice-looking guy and Nivlac wanted him and Jeanie to get married. Dwayne tolerated a lot of stuff from Jeanie. Still was trying to stick it out despite her new acclaimed drug problem. One day as his things continued to come up missing, Jeanie and Dwayne would argue over why she takes his things. At first, Dwayne and Nivlac didn't know what was going on until she started staying out all night. Dwayne and Nivlac both would worry about Jeanie and look for her all the time. Nivlac spent many nights crying and attempting suicide because he didn't understand why his mom would leave for days and nights and not contact him. This was very hurtful and Nivlac challenged the DEVIL one day.

Crying days after days and not knowing where his mother was. And how can he be so close to her and she left him. Nivlac was a momma's boy he slept in his mom's bed until he was fourteen even though he had his own room. She wanted her son next to her all the time so that bond was so hard to detach for Nivlac because he went from watching TV all night with his mother to watching the door and windows to see if she was going to come home. Nivlac will never forget the day he realized drugs was involved. She started stealing things from Dwayne and Nivlac and selling them for drugs. Dwayne was a good person and he stuck it out for about four to five years. Dwayne moved them to Muskegon Mich. To attempt to get them away from that drug scene. Sooner than later Dwayne could not take no more and left. Nivlac was stuck being an adult at thirteen and getting food from his

Granny's house or Ralph would drop off a few dollars. Literally a few dollars nothing over eighty dollars ever, but that was good to Nivlac some people didn't get that. Nivlac wanted to go live with Ralph so bad but he or Bernice said NO at the time until his mom moved back to Muskegon and Nivlac had to finish middle school. After missing so many days at school and losing focus Nivlac was held back two school years, so he finishes school while still living with his dad and stepmom. It was cool, and Nivlac lived with them for four months to complete middle school. From there, he went on to live with his Aunt Mandy for a while but ended up living with Ralph and Bernice to finish middle school.

Nivlac got close to Bernice and she was nice. Nivlac stayed in the basement and went to his Granny's or Aunt Mandy's on the weekends. Bernice was a big complainer and Nivlac was scared to leave a glass in the sink or a towel on the floor she was anal about keeping things super clean.

Nivlac moved back to Muskegon with his mom and Dwayne, He stayed the summer and they would drive to Grand Rapids to visit. But of course, Jeanie would get stuck or couldn't be found when it's time to go, so Dwayne would leave her and Nivlac. He wanted to stay and wait for Jeanie, but he would leave and eventually, come back and get them. Occasionally, Dwayne would invite Nivlac's cousin Mickey to come for a while so Nivlac wouldn't be alone. Nivlac and his cousin Mickey were like best friends and did a lot together. On this particular day Nivlac and Mickey went to the store or was playing outside. In addition, when they returned to their apartment, Nivlac noticed his mom had taken his video and video games and other items.

Nivlac was so hurt and didn't understand how she can do drugs in a whole other city, where they hardly know anyone, but low and behold she found her way. Nivlac was filled with rage he went and cut all her dresses up and stabbed all the pictures. Nivlac cousin Mickey was looking at him like OMG boy you are crazy. Nivlac was so hurt and wanted a normal life but that was not God's plan for him. Nivlac remembers he would pray for God to challenge him on something. Nivlac was so much stronger than his Mother was and knew he had an anointed spirit. In addition, he wanted the devil to try to get him addicted to anything in place of her. Nivlac would tell the devil to fuck with him Nivlac bet he would survive because he knew the Lord. Nivlac's mom taught him how to pray as a child. Nivlac was very consistent in getting on his knees to pray, and he knows a few different prayers. No one ever suspected Nivlac was going through this, because he hid this part of his life and never told others. The few that did know were family or close friends, who witnessed Jeanie's change of behavior.

Chapter 6

The Half and the Half Not Siblings

Nivlac sister, is the same age as him, their four months apart. She is so pretty and chocolate Nivlac thought she was a Black Princess. The relationship between them was rivalries at first. They would talk about each other's mothers when they were children because they share the same father. Nivlac is his father's Jr. and his only son. Nivlac and his sister Oranges spent some weekends and holidays together. They never lived in the same home, which caused rival or attention for love from their father. When Nivlac was a teenager he remembers him and Oranges seeing each other in the streets, bars, malls, etc. and she would not even acknowledge him sometime. People still don't know they're sister and brother. Nivlac was teased by his sister because Ralph favored her more, and Oranges could not wait to rub something in Nivlac's face about how Ralph did this and did that. One day on Nivlac's birthday, Ralph bought Oranges jewelry or something significant that she could rub in Nivlac's face. Nivlac would never show any emotion but deep inside it bothered him and killed his soul that a parent could favor one over the other.

When Nivlac0 was coming into his adulthood, good student never been in trouble, don't drink or smoke he was destined to show them he can obtain his own things. Not saying that Nivlac didn't receive any benefits from Ralph, but it was clear he would never be Oranges. After crying many nights not being close to either parent Nivlac continued to turn to God.

When Oranges would do bad things and go to

jail Nivlac still was a good son. Nivlac was not perfect by far but was trying to be a responsible adult because he had to grow up way before his time. Oranges loves Nivlac but it was never any real bonding time as kids, and as adults, their relationship is better, but not where it should be as sister and brother. Nivlac once had information on Oranges boyfriend and never opened his mouth that he was bisexual because he didn't want that to disrupt his relationship with his sister. When Oranges learned that Nivlac knew about her boyfriend's sexuality, she was pissed. How can Nivlac keep this information from his sister, Nivlac felt it was not his story to tell until he was for sure it was true? Nivlac found out himself the allegations of her boyfriend being bisexual was true. Nivlac loves his sister Oranges and he tell her almost everything as they are now working towards a better bond.

Pineapple is Nivlac's younger sister who is also very pretty and chocolate she favors Ralph, yet all of Ralph's children resemble him in some way. Pineapple and Nivlac were close when he lived in the home with Bernice and Ralph for the four months to complete middle school. Nivlac and Pineapple would laugh, dance and watch movies all the time. Nivlac's room was in the finished basement part of the home with a very creepy bathroom. When Bernice and Ralph were away, Nivlac and Pineapple would play loud music and run all over the house.

Once becoming an established adult with a good job, Nivlac would pick Pineapple up to stay the weekends with him and his other girl cousins. Nivlac loves his younger sister and was excited about a fresh start to a new relationship with this new sister. He use to take Pineapples on trips and loves it when she calls him brother. As time went on Nivlac and

Pineapple became distant because Nivlac was living his life and Pineapple was surviving middle school. Nivlac start to notice how much Pineapple was acting more and more like her mother Bernice, and Nivlac immediately feared that he and Pineapple's relationship would suffer. One day Nivlac was walking in the city and saw Pineapple with Bernice's best friend Gandy, and they looked at him and kept riding without even a horn hunk. Nivlac couldn't believe his sister wouldn't speak to him. Nivlac went back into self-love mode when he realized his institution regarding his relationship with Pineapple was no longer close and there was no hope for them to be close. As the years went by, Nivlac and Pineapple would still interact at family gatherings and other random encounters, but Nivlac will never forget their bond.

Pineapple was having a baby and Nivlac once again was so excited to finally have a biological niece. Nivlac would babysit every so often, and he became close with his new niece's father Duck. Duck was cool and he sometimes would hang out with Nivlac. Nivlac was hopeful his connection with Duck would somehow get him back close with Pineapple and ultimately close to his niece. Unfortunately, when Pineapple and Duck, things between Nivlac and Pineapple went back to the way they were no longer close. Nivlac was again disappointed with Pineapple during the time he loss his Granny. When Nivlac's Granny passed, Pineapple sent him a text, which read: "I'm SORRY about your grandmother." Yes, Pineapple is younger than Nivlac and he assumed because of that she did not know any better but knowing how much he loved his Granny and how close he was to her, Nivlac felt Pineapple's text was very disrespectful. Nivlac loves his younger sister and hopefully one day they will find that bond again. Nivlac is not the perfect brother but is open to fostering good relationships, especially with family.

Apple is Nivlac's stepsister and is very pretty with the same light skin complexion as Nivlac. Some assume they were biological sister and brother. Apple lived with her mother Bernice and stepfather Ralph when she and Nivlac met. Apple is not only pretty, she is funny too. She and Nivlac's bond at one time was the strongest of his three sisters. Nivlac would make her laugh and sometimes they would double team Oranges. Apple would always hang out with Nivlac and Oranges and go on trips as a family. Nivlac remember when they all went on their first family trip it was only ever two in his lifetime. They were in Louisiana and Nivlac and Oranges were talking about each other's mothers and got a butt whooping they will never forget. Apple must have teased them for years to come.

Apple then got pregnant at a young age and was very much so into hustlers at that time. She dated major hustlers and some professional boxers. When Nivlac tried to relocate to Atlanta, he ended up moving in with Bernice and Ralph for a few weeks. Then Apple needed help (allegedly) according to Bernice with paying the bills. So, Nivlac moved in with Apple and his first step niece for about two months. Everything was good! Apple and Nivlac were hanging out and acting like biological sister and brother. Until one day Apple was dating an undercover drug user who allegedly stole some of Apple's jewelry. Apple assumed one of Nivlac's friends went into her room and took jewelry. This was far from the truth, and Nivlac was falsely accused of being disloyal and an accessory to the theft. Nivlac moved out of Apple's place and tried to defend his name. Eventually, Apple and everyone else learned the truth and discovered it was Apple's boyfriend who stole the jewelry for drugs. Apple never rendered an apology to Nivlac, and this situation tarnished their relationship. Since then Nivlac and Apple hold a little animosity toward each other.

Nivlac's hurt from being accused of stealing from Apple and never receiving an apology led to retaliation. Nivlac decided to share Apple's secret wedding location information with family member. Nivlac always tried to be neutral but when you play dirty, you never win. Apple engaged to Nivlac's cousin's baby father, and all the while, this dude was threatening Nivlac's cousin, and trying to live in two households, so that he could have them both. Nivlac and Apple's relationship is never going to be the same but there's always hope for the future.

Bernice is Nivlac's stepmother who is also

very beautiful and Nivlac always wanted her to be his second Mom. She has class and is the devil's advocate when it comes to the relationships of Ralph's children. Bernice worked at a department store when she and Ralph met. Bernice is years younger than Ralph is but is a very good cook, wife, and friend to some. Not the best stepmother and not the worst, Nivlac and Bernice was close at one point all Nivlac's friends love Bernice and they call her a Diva. Nivlac and Bernice had their own relationship outside of the norm; she even got him a job at the department store where she worked. Nivlac enjoyed this part-time job and was making very good money there. On top of his main job. Bernice would try to fit in with the upper class white women there and brag on her house, car, jewelry, etc. and rightfully so because Bernice received plenty of nice gifts from Ralph.

Nivlac always had a nice apartment home and Bernice would come hang out and laugh with him and his friends. Bernice would change personalities so much it was hard to keep up with her identities. Nivlac notice how Bernice would go without speaking to Nivlac when Nivlac need something from his father. For example, Nivlac would call or come over because he need help with a car repair. Bernice would roll her eyes and get upset whenever Nivlac needed something from his father. To the point, they got into a big falling out one day. Nivlac had stored some of his clothes and personal items in the basement. When Nivlac came to get his things, Bernice said to him, "Hurry up and get these damn sissy teddy bears out my house!" Nivlac always tried to respect her but this was the last time she would be rude to him. Nivlac cursed her completely out and cursed her friend out too. "How dare you speak to me like that in my house!" Bernice screamed. Nivlac screamed back, "FUCK YOU BITCH and it's not your house!" Filled with rage Nivlac called his seven aunts to come whoop Bernice ass. Bernice claim she wasn't scared but Nivlac's aunts her his protectors and they don't play about their nephew. Ralph arrived and didn't say anything about what's going on to Nivlac. So Nivlac continued to move his items into his new place. Bernice has some good qualities but can be very rude and then suddenly get amnesia. Bernice is an acquired taste and continues to have a disconnection with Nivlac.

Years have gone by and Nivlac still tries to hold on to the good qualities that Bernice has, but not for one second like a Lion going after prey will he give her any more passes to be disrespectful. Hopefully one day they can repair their relationship. Nivlac wants to go on Iyanla Vanzant, "Fix My Life" show to repair some unresolved issues.

Nivlac's father Ralph is a real standup guy, he is the backbone of his mother's family. Ralph played sports in school and he's a real lady's man. Ralph was a hard worker and loved having nice Cadillac's. Ralph also served in the military and upon his discharge from active duty, he secured a great job working for one of the largest automotive companies in the U.S. Ralph would call Nivlac "lil bugger" and that made him feel special. Overall Nivlac appreciates his father being a nice person who always look out for his family. Ralph worked two jobs most of his life and Nivlac would visit his father at those jobs every so often to retrieve money. Ralph taught Nivlac to get a job and take care of himself. Nivlac feels like his father wanted him to follow in his footsteps and land some million-dollar job as he did, but instead Nivlac had to work and put himself through school most of his adulthood.

Nivlac was as independent as his situation would allow, and when he was ready to purchase his second car (his first car he bought from a crackhead for $80), Ralph linked him with someone who was selling a car, but the car needed a new engine. Nivlac purchased the car, rebuilt the engine, sold the car and made a profit. Then Ralph took Nivlac to buy a car and the one he wanted was going for two thousand dollars and it was better than the last car. Nivlac needed two thousand dollars in cash, and since Ralph wasn't going to help pay for the car, Nivlac hustled up on the money he needed and quickly had two thousand dollars in cash. Ralph asked Nivlac where got the money so fast and Nivlac lied to Ralph and explained that his Granny gave him a lottery number and he won two thousand dollars, but the truth is Nivlac sold drugs and worked to get that money. Nivlac has consistently seen how his father favored his sisters over him and Nivlac never said anything. Nivlac recalls a time when him and his sisters made a pack to ask their father for a thousand dollars each, and money would help the four of them get ahead. Nivlac never received his thousand dollars but the sisters did. Ralph always told his daughters, nieces and nephews he loved them publicly never showed Nivlac that same affection, only over the phone twice in life. People say all the time, "Oh that's the past." What the fuck does that really mean? Just because a person reaches adulthood, they're suppose to forgive and forget how their parents made them feel. Hell NO, this is unacceptable all children are supposed to be loved and treated equally. The past has a lot to do with the present when it comes to neglect, pain, and shame. Ralph is a good dad and has made sacrifices for his family, and Nivlac wish he was closer to Ralph, but their chemistry is off the love is there.

Nivlac's mother Jeanie has always been very beautiful and she was a beauty queen for Ms. Pontiac, Michigan. Her hair was so silky and nice people would tell her all the time I would die to have your hair. Jeanie was the oldest of twelve children; she was a substitute teacher until a fourth-grade student broke her nose at Dickerson Elementary School. After that, Jeanie begin working for a company called Keller Brown.

Jeanie prayed for Nivlac to be successful and not be caught up in making bad mistakes. She had Nivlac at twenty-two years of age and he was her first child. She was so sick during the whole pregnancy Nivlac was blessed to make it into this world, which is why he's a "chosen vessel." Jeanie got pregnant twice right after Nivlac, but both pregnancies ended with abortion. Sadly, enough, both babies would have been Ralph's, yet he paid for both abortions, and Jeanie's sister Melia drove her to Detroit for both procedures. Jeanie never expressed her desire of wanting more kids, but by Ralph not wanting any more kids and her being sick while pregnant was more than likely the reason for her abortions.

Jeanie was a very independent woman she had a nice job and had sued her a company for a lot of money. She generously shared her windfall with Ralph, which was stupid in Nivlac's opinion. Ralph was Jeanie's first boyfriend and they were together throughout high school, but their relationship dissolved when they became adults. Jeanie had several other wealthy boyfriends that made her lifestyle very nice. She would tell Nivlac all the time I have class. One day Jeanie got sick and had to have an operation and during her recovery from the operation, Jeanie said, "The pain was unbearable." This was about to be a lifestyle change, and Jeanie didn't know what she was about to encounter. Jeanie's friend introduced her to a substance she assumed would help with her pain and give her a high. This substance was very addictive, and once Jeanie tried it, life took a swift change for the worst. Jeanie and Nivlac begin to lose everything and were put out of housing. Nivlac was too young to even know what was happening he would cry and be alone a lot while she was out doing her thing.

Nivlac recalls a time when both parents were pulling each of his arms in the driveway saying, "He's coming with me." They tugged Nivlac back and forth, then eventually Ralph let go and Nivlac was granted to stay with his mother. Nivlac started to wonder why the lifestyle suddenly changed, and it took years for him to figure out that this substance had taken his mom from him. Holidays were not the same he would have fewer toys, clothes, and items. Nivlac ran away one Christmas because he didn't get anything but stuff from the Goodwill. He was devastated he wanted nothing to do with Goodwill charity. Nivlac had become so accustomed to new nice things from Sears and other popular name brand department stores. As Jeanie and Nivlac moved around life got worse. Nivlac would cry to God, "How you can let this happen to my mother?" Nivlac would be in a rage and challenge the devil. Nivlac would yell to the devil, "Come on devil try me, and try to take over my mind, body, and soul." Nivlac knew he was a much stronger person than his mother was and wanted to free her from that sickness and put that burden on him.

The devil did accept Nivlac's challenge, but God did answer his prayers and Jeanie has been substance-free for years, has since remarried a doctor, and is living a good life. Jeanie and

Nivlac have been trying to repair their relationship, but with thirty years lost without his mother, it's hard for Nivlac to get back to that place he was as a child. Jeanie spoils Nivlac even though he's an adult she still calls him her baby and gives him allowances. Nivlac believes she's trying to make up for the lost time.

Granny aka Nivlac's grandmother is a moniker Nivlac got from an old western show he watched with his grandmother. Granny is Jeanie's mother and the three of them (Jeanie, Nivlac and Granny) have the same mole located on their inner thigh. Granny was Nivlac's everything and this lady has always been his savior since birth. He loves his Granny more than anything in the world. She was a great woman, cook and life coach. Granny had a big heart but was not a pushover. Granny and Nivlac both share the same zodiac sign Sagittarius. She was a retired schoolteacher with twelve children. Nivlac had a big family and Granny owned houses and restaurants. She was a self-made woman and Nivlac spent a lot of time at his Granny's house.

Granny's house was not like theirs it was more urban, but it was fun. Everyone would come to Granny's house to laugh, drink, eat or just hangout. Granny would take in anybody, and Nivlac never understood why she would allow so many people live in her house. Granny married Billie Cox who ultimately became Nivlac's favorite Granddad, because he treated Nivlac like he was one of his own. He would always tell Nivlac to look at the hips, (talking about looking at women's asses). Billie loved Nivlac, and he was Billie's favorite and Nivlac could do no wrong in granddaddy's eyes, he could get away with murder and Billie (Granddaddy) would still protect him. Granny and Nivlac were close he shared a lot with his Granny. She showed him how to cook, and some of her secret recipes.

Granny showed Nivlac how to hustle and survive for himself. She never whooped him or was mean to him, Granny always favored Nivlac. Once Nivlac moved to Atlanta the only person he worried about back home was his Granny, and maybe a few other family members. Nivlac would call Granny and cry about his mother all the time hoping she could help her become herself again. Nivlac's grandparents taught him to never disrespect his elders it at a young age. Nivlac would visit his Granny in Michigan and loved it when she'd send him to the store to pick up her prescriptions. Nivlac made sure she was alright. Granny started getting sick and was in and out of the hospital with a few scares. In 2017 Granny passed and Nivlac was devastated, as he was just visiting her in Grand Rapids a week prior to her death. Nivlac still talks to her every day he knows she watches over him. Nivlac would love to join her in Heaven but it's up to God to say when it's time to reunite with his Granny.

Chapter 7

450 Gilbert

Nivlac has found self-love in many ways, as his Uncle Richard would say all the time, **"It will be all over in the morning."** (Gospel song). Uncle Richard had charm and a smile that made all the girls love him. He was dark-skinned, very attractive and he was just a few years older than Nivlac. Nivlac loved his Uncle Richard.

Richard was not Nivlac's blood uncle; he was Granddaddy Billie's son. Richard would come to visit in the summer and some winters, he lived in Detroit with his mother. During Nivlac's senior year in high school, he was informed that his Uncle Richard was in a bad car accident. The accident changed Uncle Richard and he was much different than the last time he visited Nivlac and the family in Grand Rapids. Around the time of the accident, Richard had to be in his early twenty's and Nivlac was nineteen. When Richard came back to Grand Rapid to visit, he was acting out, drinking and wanted to go see guys. Nivlac was confused because Richard always liked women, and Nivlac witnessed Richard having sex with a lot of women, so he was confused about how and why Richard suddenly liked men. People said it's because of the car accident that Richard changed.

Richard came to live with Aunt Mandy his biological sister, which is one of Nivlac favorite aunts. Richard had a smell that was not normal, which gave Nivlac a scare and caused him to worry about Richard. Richard would ask Mandy's husband to take him to the gay bar because he didn't want to go alone. Nivlac was too young and didn't want any parts of whatever Richard was trying to do. Nivlac went back home to his Granny's house and a few days later Richard went back to Detroit. A few months later the family received a phone call that Richard had AIDS. This was devastating to the family, they were so uneducated in the 1990s on what AIDS is. People back then said it was a GAY disease.

Nivlac was invited to travel with his Grandparents, Aunt Melia and Aunt Candy to Detroit to see Richard. Upon their arrival the doctor explained that Richard wasn't doing too well and was looking bad. The last night Richard was in Grand Rapids he stayed with his in the same house as Nivlac (Granny's house). Nivlac sensed something was wrong with Richard and was very frightened so Nivlac propped something up against his bedroom door that night so Richard would not be able to come in. When Nivlac went into the hospital with the family, he knew something was contagious.

The nurses told the family they could not see Richard unless they dress in full garments and face masks. It was highly contagious in Richard's room. Aunt Melia went in and started crying, and that made Nivlac curious, so he went in and regretted it for the rest of his life the memory of seeing Uncle Richard laying there looking like death was very hurtful. His hair was thin, and his body was 75 percent less body weight than he had a few months ago. Richard died a few days later and it was very sad. Nivlac lost one of his favorite uncles who was close in age and a protector. Richard had a good singing voice and sang, "It would be all over in the morning." all the time!

450 Gilbert aka Granny's house, was a three bedroom, two baths, with a very creepy attic, where about five to eleven people lived there

consistently. Granny fed everybody and took care of her family. Nivlac loved his Granny so much she was more than his Granny she was his Angel. Nivlac had to become a man at such a young age. 450 Gilbert is a house where so many memories where made. Nivlac's mom would come and go from 450 Gilbert and Nivlac would be so sad to see her living everywhere but was grateful when she made her way back to 450 Gilbert to sleep at Granny's house.

Nivlac desired to be different than his family and he understood what was necessary to be that change. Nivlac felt that being a hood rat was not in him. He was tired of seeing people get money from selling drugs, while he struggled to get what he could from his Granny and Ralph to survive.

During Nivlac's senior year in high school, his attitude was "fuck this" and he linked up with a friend who partnered with him to purchase a quarter of cocaine. Nivlac and his new business partner cooked up the dope and doubled their money quickly. Nivlac and his friend were kids trying to get easy money and was very easy, so easy one would ever believe that Nivlac started selling drugs.

Nivlac starting to buy cars, jewelry, clothes and a lot of furniture for his apartment. He put a lot of stuff in storage and would hide money and dope in the storage unit off 18th street. He was getting money from selling drugs and from the drug dealers who were DL (down low) that treated him as their secret. Nivlac didn't realize these DL dealers were attracted to him, but he would rent them cars and movies, they became his secret and he was theirs. These men were people boyfriends, husbands, and brothers, but Nivlac never revealed their names.

Ninety-five percent of Nivlac's clientele was family, and with their help he was rolling in the dough, and although he was robbed a few times (nothing serious), Nivlac did not stray from the mission, which was to save money and move the hell out of the ghetto at age nineteen. Nivlac's short-lived drug dealing career ended the day he started working in a restaurant called Bally's Hamburgers.

Chapter 8

What Lies Beneath

Ballys was Nivlac's first full-time job, when Nivlac started working at Ballys. He met a guy named Chuck and he seemed cool, but then Nivlac discovered that Chuck was attracted to him and it grossed him out a bit. Nivlac was accustomed to a lifestyle of DL/Trade boys, and he thought Chuck was too. Nivlac didn't know you're supposed to like your kind. He quickly invited Chuck to be his play brother, and Chuck was cool with that relationship. Chuck had several friends who Nivlac heard was also that way.

One day when Nivlac and Chuck were in Meijer's on 18th street, they ran into a group of Chuck's friends who invited him and Nivlac to hang out. Nivlac was open to meeting Chuck's friends but was scared and nervous at the same time.

Nivlac accompanies Chuck to meet up with his friends and at first Nivlac was shy but loosened up more as Chuck's friends begin talking about Detroit and the city's all-black clubs. The more they talked about the clubs, the more curious Nivlac became about whether the clubs where straight or gay. Turns out the clubs they were talking about were gay clubs and they invited Nivlac and Chuck to hang out with them in Detroit one weekend.

Nivlac, Chuck and his friends head to Detroit for the weekend. Chuck and Nivlac made a promise that if they got in this club underage and they like the club, then they're gay. When they arrive to Heaven's (the club), they stood by each other, like glue and dressed similar (lol). As Nivlac and Chuck were having the time of their lives in Heaven's, Nivlac saw a guy who reminded him of the straight boys from back home, and he wanted to meet him, so one of Chuck's friends introduced Nivlac to the guy and his name was Demonte from Muskegon, Michigan. Nivlac and Demonte chatted, and group danced. By the end of the evening, Nivlac learned that Demonte owned a fancy car and had hotel room nearby at the Marriot. Nivlac and Chuck were so tired from partying all night and before they knew it, 5:00a.m. Snuck up on them and it was time to go.

Nivlac realized that Demonte was into him when he invited Nivlac back to his hotel room. Nivlac did not want to leave Chuck and would only accept Demonte's invite if Chuck was welcomed, since Chuck's friends had left and went to stay overnight with some of their local Detroit friends. Demonte welcomed Chuck to sleep on the sofa but invited Nivlac into his bed.

Long story short, this night introduced Nivlac to whole other lifestyle and it was time for him to make major life modifications. Nivlac finished high school, found an apartment and moved out of his Granny's house.

Subsequently, Nivlac moved into his first apartment at age nineteen. His first place was fully furnished and everything right down to the silverware was brand new. Nivlac was happy all the drug dealers started to get locked up and he was into this new lifestyle and that old life faded away. Nivlac lived on his own from then on, but from time to time, his cousin Mickey lived with him.

Once Nivlac had a few thousand in the bank, he was ready to upgrade his living quarters and that is when him and his best friend Thorey visited an apartment complex in the suburbs to look for Nivlac a new apartment. To his surprise, he got approved for the first apartment he looked at. Nivlac was so happy and excited he asked the leasing agent how much his rent would be for one year she quoted him $5,400 or $4,700 something like that. Nivlac pulled from his pocket, one-year worth of rent money in cash and attempted to hand it to the leasing agent. Neither the leasing agent nor Nivlac's bestie Thorey knew it was drug money combined with legit money Nivlac earned while working at Bally's restaurant. The leasing agent immediately refused the large sum of cash and advised Nivlac to obtain a money order, and only then would they be able to finalize paperwork for his new residence. Nivlac looked at the leasing agent with confusion, as this was new to him, but without hesitation, he got the money order and it was goodbye hood life and hello suburbs!

Since living on his own at the young age of nineteen, Nivlac has been responsible to ensure his bills were always paid on time, no utilities were ever cut off, and he has never faced eviction. Nivlac made it his life mission to evolve and keep his mother's standards of having class and the finer things in life. In keeping his mother's legacy, Nivlac bought his first house at age twenty-seven, and with the help of his uncles helping paint, hammer, reshape and rebuild, it became more than a house, it was a home.

The years of living in the hood for Nivlac was finally over. However, living in the ghetto was life changing and presented many teachable moments, which makes Nivlac very grateful. Nivlac will forever embrace everything he learned living in the hood, such as; the culture, the struggle, how to hustle, how the street life increased his street smarts and the education system kept him book smart. Nivlac has a giving heart and some say he's mean but that's just a cover-up. The ones who get close to him know the real him and its very few. His Aunt Melia always told him don't trust anybody ever. And this is Nivlac's model until this day, don't trust anybody and everybody is not your friend.

Chapter 9

The New Change

Nivlac finally got the nerve to hang out at an (alternative club) in Grand Rapids. He was so scared even though he knew what the club was about. Fact is, Nivlac lived a straight life but he was always curious. The one day he gets the courage to check out the alternative club, he runs into Amber in the parking lot. Just so happens the alternative club shares a parking lot with a popular Mexican restaurant frequented mostly after people leave nightclubs in the area. Amber is one of Nivlac uncle's girlfriends, so he refers to her as Aunt Amber. Well, Aunt Amber saw Nivlac leaving the alternative club and kept watching him until he was out of her sight.

Amber didn't waste any time telling Nivlac's Granny that she saw him at the alternative club. Within a few days, Granny called Nivlac to inquire about what she'd heard from Amber, and to remind Nivlac of how his Uncle Richard died. Granny basically, shared her thoughts about that lifestyle being bad and how living that way results in AIDS and ultimately death. Granny commanded Nivlac to stay away for the alternative club and in many ways commanded he avoid that lifestyle all together. After his Granny's devastating call, Nivlac cried and immediately slipped into depression. Nivlac had a close friend who was obsessed with him. This friend was going to marry a female until he met Nivlac. Nivlac needed advice, so he called this guy friend because he was more experienced in the lifestyle and could give Nivlac the advice and comfort he was seeking.

Nivlac's friend comforted him by buying Nivlac a big black cute teddy bear. Nivlac named the bear COCO CHANEL, and COCO soon became Nivlac's go to, as he cried many nights on COCO. Nivlac decided to learn more about the lifestyle and once he did, he was no longer ashamed of who he was. The DL (down low), trade guys was a new thing to him. It was like he inherited some new power and knowledge from the alternative elders. With this new-found knowledge and power, Nivlac had the DL and trade guys in the palm of my hands.

Nivlac could write a whole other book on how many supposedly straight guys, married guys, DL guys, drug dealing guys and trade guys who's tried to have sex with him or talk to him, because he's had his share of that closeted behavior.

Nivlac loved the money his closeted friends would give him, and unlike other alternative guys, Nivlac is all about the money or what one brings to the table. If they're not talking about money or what they can do for him they're not his type (PERIOD.T). Regardless of his friend's choice to stay closeted, to this day Nivlac remains silent out of respect for their personal choice, so if you're reading this book don't worry, you shall remain nameless.

Nivlac's theory is maybe there is a ten percent population of guys who will not engage with other guys, but the other ninety percent will, whether its curiosity, money or they're simply bisexual.

Chapter 10

Grown and Sexy

Nivlac is now twenty-four years old, living life, working and embracing his new lifestyle. Nivlac has always been accustomed to the finer things in life, so the lifestyle he's made for himself affords him the finest clothes, nice car, and his dwelling place is always the perfect image of a model home like in a magazine. Nivlac's continued success caused people to be jealous, but it didn't bother him, because he was determined to pick up where his mom left off, and that meant living lavishly.

Nivlac's personality naturally magnetic causing people to gravitate toward him, but on the flip side, his attitude is not to be tampered with. At age twenty-four, everything in Nivlac's life is good and he knows he is the "shit!"

Nivlac started dating E.H. while also in the process of moving back into his own place. Nivlac had been on his own since he was nineteen, and for people to treat him like he's a bum or never had his own was unacceptable to him, especially since it was his burn incident that caused him to live with others while he recovered.

Nivlac returned to his former job in Grand Rapids, saved his money, bought enough new furniture to furnish an entire house and then he and E.H. decided to move in together. This was Nivlac's first time living with someone he dated, but E.H. loved Nivlac and it was evident because he accepted all Nivlac's flaws.

Nivlac got his mojo back through self-love and he was back to being himself. His scars were healing, and it had been two years since his burn incident. It wasn't unusual for Nivlac to bounce back so quickly since he's an only child, and there have been many times where he had to fend for himself and look out for himself.

Nivlac's had his first break up and fall out when his first real boyfriend told him he slept with his best friend Thorey. Nivlac was devastated, he didn't ask for that betrayal and nor did he deserve it. If it's one thing Nivlac learned growing up in the hood it's that "loyalty" is the TRUTH! Nivlac put the pieces of his broken heart back together through self-love and he became stronger, better and allowed his strength will lead the way.

At twenty-eight years of age, Nivlac bought his first house. At this time, he had a great job working at a nutrition company, and the pay was more than generous. However, the company begin downsizing and were firing people left and right. One day, Nivlac made a mistake that was common amongst Team Leads, but not nearly as big of a mistake, as some of the other fuck-ups he had seen. Unfortunately, instead of speaking to a supervisor about his mistake, Nivlac tried to correct it himself, and a few days later, he was terminated without a written or verbal warning. To be honest, he surprisingly felt a sense of relief. Yes, the job at the nutrition company paid good money, but Nivlac's desire to finish college was seemingly possible since he'd lost his job.

Nivlac decided to sell his house and give Atlanta another try. He was determined to educate himself and obtain a degree. He did it four years and now he holds a Bachelor of Business Administration with a concentration in International Affairs.

Chapter 11

Face to Face

When you think your life could not get any worse, then the doctor pronounced you blind and says your face is fractured for life.

One day as Nivlac was leaving his condominium after returning from a trip to Detroit with friends, there was a lot of construction work happening on his street. Nivlac approached the construction workers to inquire about the route residents should travel when leaving the subdivision. They instructed him on which route to take, and so for the next few days he took the route given by the construction workers.

Nivlac and his friends love going to the malls and restaurants together. It's their bonding and fun friend time. One day Nivlac and his friends met up at his condominium, and then headed out to eat, and Nivlac drove his vehicle. As Nivlac followed the route given by the construction workers, he was struck by another car and his face hit the windshield. Nivlac was rushed to the hospital in an ambulance, and everything was a blur he felt excruciating pain in his face and he also felt like the bones in his face were dislocated.

The news of Nivlac's accident traveled quickly and when Nivlac arrived at the hospital, the entire waiting room was filled with his mother's side of the family, along with his mother Jeanie, Ralph and Bernice. The doctors immediately searched the waiting room for Nivlac's parents because some decisions had to be made. Once his parents were identified, they went into the hospital room and the doctor delivered the bad news.

"Nivlac you have fractured the right side of your face and if we don't do the surgery you could end up with a disfigured face." Nivlac was in shock to say the least and extremely devastated at how bad things keep happening to him while he's trying to live right, and treat people right, yet bad things happen.

The doctor asked probing questions to gain a better understanding of Nivlac's medical history, so they could proceed with PLASTIC SURGERY. The doctor also shared, there was a possibility Nivlac could go blind in one eye because it was necessary to go through his mouth and one of his eyes to perform the plastic surgery. In addition to that, the doctor explained it was necessary to place metal plates in his face in order to maintain facial structure.

Nivlac was so hurt and in so much pain. After discussing his options with his parents, he decided to proceed with the surgery. Nivlac endured several hours of plastic surgery to his face which costed approximately $46,000. After surgery, Nivlac could not breathe on his own, so the doctors kept him in recovery until he no longer needed the breathing machine. Nivlac's father Ralph was at his bedside encouraging him to breathe by speaking positive affirmations to Nivlac, saying, "Come on boy you can do it." Hearing those words from his father gave Nivlac the will he needed, and he did it. Nivlac was happy to see his father at his side this time, because he recalls no one being there at the hospital in Atlanta when he was in the Burn Unit.

Nivlac's mom Jeanie was also waiting in the room for him, and she stayed at the hospital for a few days until Nivlac was able to talk. Everyone was worried about how Nivlac's face will turn out, because Nivlac was so into his looks. Nivlac said to himself if he doesn't look the same after the plastic surgery, he was going to kill himself, because he did not want anyone making fun of his face or injuries.

While lying in his hospital bed still recovering from the plastic surgery, Nivlac overheard his mom on the phone. Nivlac couldn't help but to wonder what was going on, as he heard the person on the phone tell him mom don't tell him, but her look gave it all away. Jeanie wanted to protect her son, but finally she informed him that while he was in surgery somebody burglarized his house.

This news was more than Nivlac could bare. He was even more devastated as to what the hell was going on. He questioned why people were attacking him and all these BAD things keep happening to him. Nivlac knew he had a good relationship with the Lord, so he was deeply hurt and confused.

Almost everything was stolen from Nivlac's condo during the burglary, while he was in the hospital. Ralph left the hospital and went with one of his friends to secure Nivlac's condo. Nivlac can't believe that while he's lying in a hospital bed in pain and recovering from a major accident, someone took that opportunity to burglarize his condo. The only solace Nivlac had in this situation is the fact he had homeowner's insurance but that's beside the point.

This is a cruel world we live in and everyone must answer for his or her wrong doings. Nivlac has never been a perfect person but he's never been a bad guy either. Nivlac has helped many people and still does. Not to mention when he first moved to Atlanta, someone burglarized his house and took everything.

Unfortunately, Nivlac will never play sports or be in any physical activity, because he has metal in his face and any disruption to the plate in his face could cause deformity.

Chapter 12
Welcome to the "A"

Atlanta the day the earth stood still, was the first day Nivlac moved to Atlanta, and it was nothing but the DEVIL who sent demons to distract his move, or it may have been God saying this is not the right move for you son.

Well, all hell broke loose when Nivlac and his friend he calls (son), was driving Nivlac's Hummer to Atlanta and was pulled over by some white cops.

The cops called the dogs and was treating Nivlac as if he was a criminal or a drug lord. Nivlac had several thousand in his safe from selling household items in Grand Rapids and owned a Hummer truck because he can afford it and what was in the safe was his personal business. Nivlac had a feeling this random police stop would go left fast, so Nivlac being the fast thinker he's always been, waited for the police officers to run their names and when the officers started to threaten them, Nivlac sat back in the truck and pushed the OnStar button. Nivlac asked OnStar to record or at the least, listen to everything that was happening between him, his friend and the police officers. When the police officers realized OnStar was listening, they backed down and let Nivlac and his friend go.

Nivlac finally arrived in Atlanta, and the movers he hired were supposed to arrive in Atlanta with his things a day or two behind his arrival. Nivlac was out on the town enjoying cocktails on his first night in the "A" when he received a phone call from the mover saying their moving truck broke down in Kentucky. Nivlac was like what!!! He was so discombobulated that he could not enjoy the rest of his night (WTF).

Nivlac was highly irritated when he recalled the fact, the moving company was a "shade tree" mover recommended by his Uncle Spider. Instead of dwelling on that, Nivlac immediately called his friend Taryn and asked for help to drive seven hours to Kentucky to get his property!

Nivlac and Taryn quickly head to Kentucky in his Hummer. Upon their arrival in Kentucky, Nivlac rented a U-Haul to transfer his items from the mover's truck to the U-Haul. As Nivlac and Taryn finished loading his items to the UHAUL, the mover asked Nivlac if he was to help get their truck fixed. The look on Nivlac face was priceless, but his acting skills kicked in and in the most convicting voice, ever Nivlac said, "Of course! Once we're back in Atlanta and if you haven't resolved truck issue, we'll come to get you and help you." "Yeah right, I'm not coming back after they were paid for half the move already! It's not my problem their truck broke down." Nivlac said to himself as he walked away to get in the U-Haul and drive back to Atlanta.

On the drive back to the "A", Nivlac drove the U-Haul and Taryn drove his Hummer. Nivlac was feeling great because he'd handled his business. Got a U-Haul to safely get his property to Atlanta, and his friend Taryn to drive his Hummer back. Then BOOM another issue arise (STRIKE THREE)! Nivlac screams out, "Oh my fucking goodness why me, why me, why me!"

Nivlac slowly trailed behind because the size and weight of the U-Haul, his speed was significantly slower than that of a Hummer. Nivlac thought he explained to the dumb bitch Taryn, how slow he'd be driving and how he can't go as fast in a big ass U-Haul. Long story short, Nivlac had to stop and get gas, and all the while, he felt exhausted and defeated especially since he's never in life had to drive this far alone. Nivlac tried to pull the U-Haul in the gas station and accidentally ran over the rail that blocks people from hitting the gas pumps. Him hitting that rail could have caused a major explosion. The rail was fucked up and the U-Haul gained a big long dent on the side from hitting the rail.

Nivlac was so happy to make it back to the "A" safe and sound. Luckily when he returned the U-HAUL the rep who checked it in didn't check the side where the dent occurred and signed off on the U-Haul. Nivlac was also lucky no one from the gas station called the police or shared camera footage of the accident. Nivlac quickly realized he had more than luck on his side, it was a blessing that the three things which tried to prevent him from relocating did not prevail. Nivlac finally became acclimated to the "A" and embraced positive changes in his life, his journey to becoming Nivlac the Brand began.

Nivlac's biggest positive change was how much the relationship between his father Ralph and his stepmother Bernice evolved to point they made sure not to miss him walk across the stage when he graduated college with his BBA in 2015. They drove from Michigan to Atlanta to celebrate his accomplishment.

Nivlac still feels very optimistic about Atlanta. He likes the fact that people from all walks of life have settled in the "A" (they call themselves imports), which are people who were not born in the "A." Nivlac has met some amazing people to include actors, singers, reality stars, etc. Nivlac has ever been star struck Nivlac and has mostly stuck on himself. His attitude toward the celebrity scene is "Fuck these people they're just regular humans.

When it comes to dating in Atlanta, Nivlac feels the dating scene is cursed, because it seems in the "A" loyalty is a thing of the past. Despite his feelings about the dating scene in the ATL Nivlac makes sure he's always READY! Well one day Nivlac made a mistake that could have cost him his life.

Not thinking straight (no pun intended lol), Nivlac was grooming himself for a pool party and he wanted the perfect shave (you know where) so, he used a razor to shave down there with the hope of looking fabulous in his swimsuit. A week or two later he noticed bumps in his genital area and realized he must have cut himself last time he shaved. Attempting to clean the bumps daily, Nivlac poured peroxide on the bumps. Within the next couple of days of using the peroxide, Nivlac woke up and his genitals were swollen up big to the size of tennis balls. Nivlac immediately went to the hospital and that's when he learned the area where he shaved had got infected with bacteria. He was hospitalized four days. The doctor explained to him that he arrived just in time, because he infection was in his bloodstream and could have killed him. Lesson learned and after that scare, Nivlac swore he would never use a razor to shave anything on his body again.

Chapter 13

Lord of the Rings Spirit of the Hidden Devil

Nivlac has now been living in Atlanta since the later part of 2009. The population in Atlanta is overpopulated with people from all over the country, and, the culture was much different from Grand Rapids, Michigan.

Nivlac is now fully acclimated to Atlanta and is ready to date again. In this instance "again" means he begin dating a person he calls Irv Gotti "again." Nivlac and Irv Gotti once lived together in Michigan, well Irv Gotti decided to move from Detroit, Michigan to be with Nivlac. Irv Gotti was an opportunist and was very nice looking. In their past relationship in Michigan, Nivlac and Irv Gotti were only together a few months because Irv Gotti couldn't seem to get himself established. Nivlac tried to stick it out with Irv Gotti until one-day Nivlac came home from work and Irv Gotti had taken a few items from Nivlac's place and some money and moved back to Detroit. Nivlac was very upset, but realized it was out of his control and had the attitude, "What can you do when it comes to people who will do anything for survival."

Since that time in Michigan when Irv Gotti stole from Nivlac, years had passed, but Irv Gotti reached out to Nivlac when he first arrived in Atlanta to apologize for his wrong doings. Nivlac forgave him and this led to Irv Gotti visiting Nivlac from time to time in Atlanta, however it didn't take long for Irv Gotti to strike again and disappear back to Detroit.

Irv Gotti could never seem to find his purpose in life. He wanted to be someone famous and thought his looks would get he there, but it never did. It's a good thing Nivlac was stable and unbothered by the shenanigans Irv Gotti pulled on him. A few more years went by and Irv Gotti surfaced again and was very apologetic to Nivlac and shared with him that he was ready to make a move to Atlanta to start a reality show. Irv Gotti was indeed charming and a people pleaser. He used all the right words but lied like a low-down dirty dog. Nivlac's good heart wouldn't allow him to say no to Irv Gotti, so he agreed to help, and let him move in with him under the condition they would just be "FRIENDS!"

Nivlac is no fool and was very careful about this move he was making with Irv Gotti. Let the LIES begin! One day Irv Gotti allegedly had interviews with celebrities and was scheduled for a cameo appearance on a show. This was the first of many lies to come and somewhere along the way, Nivlac and Irv Gotti started back having relations with the hopes of getting their relationship back to where it was long ago. At this point in life, they had both matured and seemingly had the desire to look out for each other.

The LIES continue! Irv Gotti start having different people drop him off and pick him up would explain to Nivlac that he was being transported by producers. He would show Nivlac photos of him with these "so-called" producers at the various places they visited, but Nivlac was sure Irv Gotti was playing games yet again.

Irv Gotti allegedly had a "homeless" cousin who needed a place to live, so he asked Nivlac if the two of them could help this "alleged" cousin and let him live with them. Even though Nivlac was suspicious of the "alleged" cousin, his good heart couldn't say no to the "homeless."

Nivlac's instincts kicked in and he decided to stay home from work one day to see what was really going on with Irv Gotti and his "alleged" cousin, especially since Irv Gotti begin staying out all night and was turning into a no call no show boyfriend. Nivlac's first thought was to tell Irv Gotti and his "alleged" cousin to get the fuck out, but his instinct said INVESTIGATE! Instead of parking his car in the driveway, Nivlac parked away from the house so it would appear he wasn't home.

Nivlac waited inside his alone home hoping for the best, but his gut feeling feared the worse. When Nivlac heard a car pull up in front of the house he peeked out of the window and saw a black car pull into the driveway. When he realized it was Irv Gotti his "alleged" cousin Nivlac hid in the bedroom closet to listen in on their conversation. His gut was right and within minutes, Nivlac heard Irv Gotti affectionally call his "alleged" cousin either boo or baby. Turns out, Irv Gotti's "alleged" cousin it not his relative at all and they were in fact messing around.

Nivlac could not believe what was happening! The "alleged" cousin was in the shower and Irv Gotti was laughing and flirting with him in Nivlac's house (how disrespectful is that). Nivlac was filled with rage thinking how he'd given Irv Gotti the benefit of the doubt and trusted that he was a changed man. On top of that, Nivlac trusted that Irv Gotti's "alleged" cousin was exactly that, "a relative." Nivlac's blood begin to boil the more his thoughts got the best of him, and he jumped out the closet and screamed, "Both of you lying bitches get the fuck out of my house NOW!"

Both Irv Gotti and his "alleged" cousin was in shock when Nivlac came from the closet in a rage yelling, "Who the fuck comes into someone's house and does this?" Nivlac called the police while cursing them out at the same time. The "alleged" cousin jumped out of the shower as soon as he heard Nivlac's voice. Nivlac didn't care that the "alleged" cousin was butt naked as he chased him out of the house with a knife. Irv Gotti tried to stop Nivlac and got cut in the process.

Nivlac eventually got them out of the house and was waited for the police to arrive. When the police arrived, sadly that felt Nivlac was the aggressor and he was arrested and taken to jail. Nivlac had never been to jail and was very upset! For the life of him he couldn't understand how the State of Georgia considered him the aggressor when in fact it was Irv Gotti and his "alleged" cousin who were the ones that disrespected Nivlac's home with their wrong doing.

Unfortunately, because the jail computer

systems were down at the time Nivlac was arrested, he had to spend four days in jail. When the jail computer system was restored, Nivlac was blessed to receive bail money from his cousins on his dad Ralph's side of the family totaling to approximately two thousand dollars. Ralph and Bernice paid the cousins back and sent the money needed to get Nivlac out of jail.

Nivlac was so grateful to have Ralph and Bernice come to his rescue during this situation, because for many years Nivlac felt like he never really received anything big from Ralph or Bernice, and it really made him happy that they took care of him in that way. However, Ralph and Bernice gave Nivlac a lecture about paying them back but Nivlac felt because they never paid for his education or did anything big for him, this small redemption was payback. Nivlac was thinking if they needed it or any family member needed money to get out of jail, he would do the same thing. The jail was filthy and nasty, but Nivlac asserted himself during a near breakdown and was strong. He made friends in jail by giving advice and not shying away from the thugs who were locked up with him. Of course, Nivlac wanted to be in jail because as we all know jail is not a place anyone wants to be in.

Nivlac tried to obtain a lawyer to sue Irv Gotti and the Atlanta police department, but no one would take his case. However, Nivlac did obtain a criminal lawyer to help him beat the arrest. They won his case and all charges were dropped and Nivlac still has no criminal record.

Chapter 14

Creating a New Strength

Nivlac has been through more than an average person can handle, but he refuses to give up and decided to get back to loving himself and living his life to the fullest.

In 2016 Nivlac met someone in Mississippi at a party he hosted with a few reality stars. Nivlac had no clue this person he met in Mississippi is a "hell raiser." Nivlac did a lot of socializing at the party, as well as friending people on Facebook. Most of the people at the party seemed like good country folk but turns out a lot of them were messy ASF!

How can such a small town keep up so much drama? Nivlac and "hell raiser" stayed connected after the party and engage in a distant relationship for approximately a year. Then Nivlac and "hell raiser" decided to move in together in Nivlacs townhome in Atlanta. Nivlac and "hell raiser" had good chemistry but the new person in Nivlac's life was a down-low demon. They had good days, but more bad days, and unfortunately when you're with someone you love it's easy to turn a blind eye to the fact, they're violent.

Nivlac always believed he was one of the best fighters on the face of the earth, until he came up against "hell raiser." There were times when he and "hell raiser" would attend events and have an altercation because "hell raiser" would assume Nivlac was cheating. Just from speaking to an associate or friend. One thing led to another and things would get physical and before you know it Nivlac would immediately be put out of commission before the fight began.

There was one time when "hell raiser" squeezed Nivlac's wrist so hard he fractured both wrist. Which resulted in Nivlac wearing two casts on his wrist and arms for a few months. Despite what "hell raiser" did, Nivlac still felt sorry for the situation and in actuality, he needed "hell raiser" to help him heal, feed him, wash him up, and use the restroom.

Only a few weeks had passed since the wrist incident and "hell raiser" started another physical altercation with Nivlac even though Nivlac was incapable of fighting back. Nivlac's arms were still in a cast and Nivlac felt so helpless and afraid because he knew that the only way out of this situation was DEATH and at this point, one of them had to go because enough was enough!

Nivlac was reminded of the situation that happened two years prior where he was jailed for protecting his home. He remembered how the law in the State of Georgia treated him like a criminal rather than the victim. Nivlac feared the law wouldn't protect him until it's too late and someone would either be in jail, seriously hurt, or DEAD!

"Hell Raiser" proposed to Nivlac, but the RING that was given to Nivlac as an engagement confirmation to marriage was a pure joke. Nivlac felt the RING should represent: honesty, loyalty, respect, love, compassion, monogamy, and TRUST!

The engagement for Nivlac was very serious because he thought he'd found someone who accepted his flaws, his personality, his looks, and his independence. Nivlac even went so far as to put his business (of his engagement to "hell raiser") on social media and his family now had conformation of his lifestyle. A few hours after posting the engagement on social media, Nivlac received a phone call from his father Ralph. Ralph congratulated Nivlac, told him he loves him and didn't care what gender he was marrying. Ralph ended the call with, "If you're happy, I'm happy. Everyone needs somebody." Nivlac lied at first and said his engagement was a joke just for fun on social media. Then after receiving a call right after hanging up the phone with his father from his sister Oranges. His sister asked him, "Why did you lie to our father? He doesn't care who you're with." Nivlac immediately started crying and it was tears of joy and comfort to know that his father finally acknowledges him or accepted him after all these years, especially since his father never had a conversation with him about sex or sexuality. Nivlac would sometime ask his sister and stepmom how his father felt about his lifestyle, but neither of them confirmed anything negative.

Nivlac's engagement to "hell raiser" only

last a few months as things begin to shift downhill. Nivlac had accumulated many friends and associates while living in Atlanta over the past eight years. Nivlac was known for always being the center of attention. Everyone he encounters tend to confide in him and love his personality. People naturally gravitated to Nivlac for advice and general personal conversations. Nivlac knows he is a "chosen vessel" and the demon that who lives inside "hell raiser" (his former fiancé) did not like the attention or the accomplishments that Nivlac has accumulated while only being in Atlanta for such a short time. Even though Nivlac would explain that the people they encountered were his friends who he'd known for years, "hell raiser" still found a way to destroy relationships with Nivlac and others. After a while it became overwhelming because the constant false accusations of infidelity, lack of trust and dishonesty were all made up in "hell raiser's" head. Things between Nivlac and "hell raiser" continued to become more violently physical to the point of domestic violence and after several severe incidents Nivlac ended their engagement.

Domestic violence can be verbal or physical and it applies to any gender. People need to realize it never turns out good when you're in that kind of situation (GET OUT).

Nivlac has a seventh sense that pick up on people who are not trustworthy (fake friends). It was a slap in the face, when Nivlac learned a few of his close friends had been feeding "hell raiser" false information which caused most of the rage in their relationship. Although their aim was to destroy Nivlac, God stepped in and said NOT ON MY WATCH!

Nivlac was so hurt from the breakup of his engagement and all the turmoil that came with it and went into a slight depression, but he's learned to "create his own strength" and by doing so no one ever knew what he was going through, not even his coworkers or other friends. Nivlac was so disappointment in how unfair "hell raiser" treated him after he helped "hell raiser" become a better person. Nivlac helped him get a new car, career change, lifestyle upgrade, and most importantly Nivlac truly loved "hellraiser" flaws and all.

Nivlac went back to his praying roots and got that demon off his back and stayed to himself. To rebuild confidence in who he is and what he stands for event though his first thought was to retaliate, fight or destroy, but God said, "No handle this situation a different way and let me help you!" A few weeks after the breakup of their engagement, things started to unveil, and God removed bad demons from Nivlac's life. God didn't stop there, He also allowed Nivlac to watch those who betrayed him, lose jobs, cars, and living quarters.

Nivlac is back to his normal self (thank God). He got out that dangerous situation and God removed fake friends in the process, because God only knows things could have gone another way. Nivlac is known by some of his close family what he is capable of. Back in the day when Nivlac was in high school, his Aunt Melia and her boyfriend had broken Nivlac's windshield on his car and lied about doing it. Nivlac's uncle in law told him what he and his aunt had done it after they were fighting. Nivlac grabbed some hairspray and a lighter and lit them on fire as they ran out the house yelling and screaming, "He's crazy!" Nivlac did several things out of revenge that he has no regrets over and will keep to himself. Therefore, you must be careful about how you treat people, because you never know when it's your time to pay the pied piper.

Remember if you're not happy pray about it and hit the reset button as many times as you like. You must have self-love to love anyone else. Like Nivlac's Granny use to say, "Blessed by the best!"

Back in the day there was a popular song titled: Backstabbers and the hook says, "All along they want to take your place them backstabbers." What these backstabbers didn't know is that Nivlac has dealt with jealousy, bullying, molestation, verbal/physical abuse, parent disappointments, suicide attempts, hate, spiritual challenges, drug awareness, and many other life-changing events. Nivlac has found self-love in many ways, and like his Uncle Richard use to say, "It will be all over in the morning."

Chapter 15

Don't Get Caught Up

Atlanta is a city that either consumes you or makes you successful. Nivlac has seen many come to the "A" trying to be something they're not. Atlanta is designed for blacks to succeed and is the home of one of the largest black-owned studios, Tyler Perry Studios. Atlanta has mega churches and mega clubs, bars, social scenes in the country. Nivlac has made many friends and acquaintances. Nivlac is still do some soul searching and practicing self-love as he learns to keep a balance. Nivlac's venture to Atlanta was a "faith" move to experience Atlanta's lifestyle. Nivlac has been blessed to help so many people in several different ways.

On the flip side, Atlanta can also be looked upon as one of the fakest cities in the country. People in the "A" tend to put on this facade that their more than what they are. Everyone is either a model, stylist, actor, rapper or something. Nivlac is from Michigan where people are just who they are, and no one is trying to be something they are not.

The dating scene in Atlanta is horrible there are very few consistent people. We call people who move from other places "IMPORTS" (this means they're from other cities). It takes at least two years to adjust to Atlanta. Atlanta offers so many opportunities for heterosexual, DL, homosexual, bi-sexual and all the above, so to try and find LOVE in a city filled with so many inconsistent black beautiful people feels like a CURSE.

Nivlac went to a strip club one night with his girlfriend Mykel and they were enjoying themselves. Mykel had to run to the restroom but before she went, she was telling Nivlac, look at some random guy he should talk to. The guy peeked Nivlac's interest because he looked like he had some money. As Mykel proceeded to go to the bathroom, the guy came over to Nivlac and asked to buy him a drink, and Nivlac accepted because he was a little interested as well. The introduction was made, and the guy's name is Tyrell. Turns out Tyrell was very nice Upon Mykel's return from the bathroom, she was upset and voiced to Tyrell, "Oh you bought him a drink and not me!"

Mykel was what is called hating because she wondered why the hell Tyrell was in Nivlac's face and not hers. Nivlac and Tyrell exchanged information and they became cool. Turns out Tyrell is a drug dealer and he supplies strippers. Nivlac was familiar with this kind of guy and wasn't afraid to start asking for gifts.

Tyrell and Nivlac talked for a few years and Tyrell would give Nivlac money and gifts all the time and made Nivlac think it's about damn time somebody make me feel like I'm back in Michigan. Then, of course, the nature of the drug business took over and with Tyrell being from New York, he either disappeared or got locked up. Nivlac never heard from him again, so he went back to his regularly scheduled program and remember it was fun while it lasted.

Nivlac held on to those memories of how Tyrell loved his cooking so much he was planning on opening a restaurant and Nivlac was going to run it. Once again Nivlac's personality attracts people from all walks of life, and he can adapt to anyone and any environment rather it's a trap house or the white house, he's just universal in that way.

One day while at work Nivlac met this nice family who looked like they just had a baby. The couple was very attractive, and the husband was chocolate and handsome. Nivlac greeted them both and went on with his day. Until the wife decided to go ahead and push the stroller with her child and go shopping. The husband returned to Nivlac's counter in the men's department and started asking questions about the colognes. His name was Byron and truth be told, he just wanted to hold a conversation with Nivlac.

It didn't take long for Byron to ask Nivlac for his information so he can take him out. Nivlac was nervous and feared his wife will walk up at any minute and catch them exchanging information and curse him out. She never did, Byron was nice and said to Nivlac, "Let me take you out on a date." "Ok cool not a problem." Nivlac responded. Byron sent a driver in a white on white Rolls Royce to pick up Nivlac for their date. Nivlac's eyes were excited and happy at the same time. He and Byron went out to a fine dining restaurant and had a good time, and he drove Nivlac home himself. Byron would tell Nivlac all the time he's only with the wife because they have a baby together. Nivlac and Byron started seeing each other and having fun and long talks. Byron was unhappy in his marriage but Nivlac has been in this situation several times before. Byron started being more distance with Nivlac and that ended after a couple of years. Nivlac is so used to the disappointment in relationships he's immune to it. This is when he can always count on self-love to create his own strength. Atlanta is a place where you can be all you can be or fake it until you make it, but whatever you chose to do, don't get caught up.

Epilogue

Closing Remarks

Know Your Self-worth

This book is to create awareness and hopefully touch someone that can understand or relate to this story. Nivlac is a name that can be used by anyone. Just take your name and spell it backwards if it doesn't make sense that's fine life doesn't make sense. It's your alter-ego and you can find a happy place and bury anything in your life that affects you today.

Take a deep breath, recognize your self-worth, find the good qualities you have feed off that and live for you. Don't let anyone or any circumstances hold you to the person you were (your past). You have no control over life situations that catches you like the wind blowing through your nose. Self-worth is knowing that you can apply yourself to be a better you, Nivlac always said, "People are unpredictable, and no one can foresee the things people do to others. Just try to live right by GOD and do well." Nivlac is not perfect but is a HERO for many lost souls and has an amazing anointing on his life.

Living your Best Life:

Nivlac is now focusing on what's important which is God and family. He is becoming an entrepreneur and embracing his newfound courage. Nivlac has been able to create his own strength through everything he has endured and the things he has experienced. Nivlac predicts that in 2025 he will be retired and sitting in a mansion off the water. He hopes that him and his family will continue to build their relationship and love.

Nivlac has been through so much in his adult life that he is owed something good and positive to happen to him. Nivlac started making a cookbook that has all his Granny's good dishes and taste. **Nivlac The Brand** represents: Strength and Love. The brand encourages people to follow their dreams and be open-minded. Nivlac is non-judgmental and will be creating jobs for people in the future. Remember, you too can **Create Your Own Strength.**

www.ingramcontent.com/pod-product-compliance
Lightning Source LLC
LaVergne TN
LVHW041544070426
835507LV00011B/928